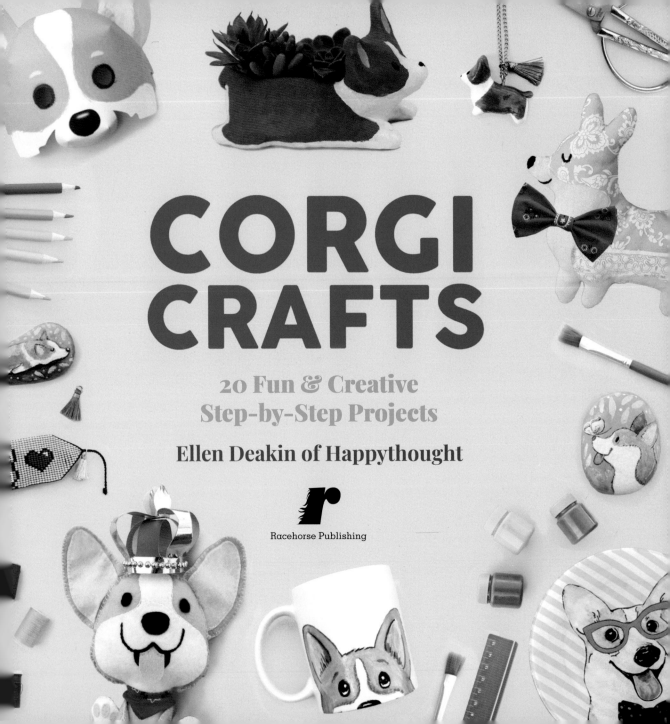

CORGI
CRAFTS

20 Fun & Creative
Step-by-Step Projects

Ellen Deakin of Happythought

r

Racehorse Publishing

Racehorse Publishing books may be purchased in bulk at special discounts for sales promotion, corporate gifts, fund-raising, or educational purposes. Special editions can also be created to specifications. For details, contact the Special Sales Department, Skyhorse Publishing, 307 West 36th Street, 11th Floor, New York, NY 10018 or info@skyhorsepublishing.com.

Racehorse Publishing™ is a pending trademark of Skyhorse Publishing, Inc.®, a Delaware corporation.

Visit our website at www.skyhorsepublishing.com

10 9 8 7 6 5 4 3 2 1

Library of Congress Cataloging-in-Publication Data is available on file.

Cover and interior design by Antonia Orrego Requena & Ellen Deakin
Cover photography by Ellen Deakin

Print ISBN: 978-1-63158-667-5
Ebook ISBN: 978-1-63158-688-0

Printed in China

CONTENTS

INTRODUCTION

Welcome to *Corgi Crafts*!
I'm so excited to share twenty-three fun and original Corgi projects.

Corgis are the cute dogs that everyone is crazy for.
From their adorable faces to their fluffy butts to their Royal connections,
Corgis are top dog when it comes to cuteness and personality.

Get crafty with these adorable Corgi-themed crafts, perfect for novice or
expert crafters. Each project comes with step-by-step photo instructions.

Everything that you will need to craft each project is listed in the
book along with templates and guides. So let's get crafting!

Ellen

*The projects in this book are rated from easy to advanced and there
is also an indication of how long each project will take.
Each project that has a template will include the rightmost icon below.*

Easy   Medium   Advanced   Time needed   Includes templates

ALL ABOUT CORGIS

Folklore about Pembroke Welsh Corgis says that fairies gave two Corgi puppies to some children in the forest, and from this our modern Corgis developed. They were said to have been the fairies' war horses. On either side of their shoulders there is a line of rougher fur with lighter markings, said to be the saddle line for fairy warriors.

Corgis were developed from dogs like the Siberian Husky and were first brought to England in the twelfth century, probably by weavers. According to the *Oxford English Dictionary*, **cor** means dwarf and **gi** means dog. They measure about twelve inches in height at the shoulder level. They came to be used as herding dogs but now are more usually found as pets.

For many, Corgis have a royal connection. The British queen, Elizabeth II, had a Corgi as a pet when she was a child, and has continued to love them all her life. She has owned thirty or more Corgis during her life.

CHARACTERISTICS

Corgis have a foxy face, large triangular ears, short legs, and traditionally a short tail, although today the practice of docking the tail to make it short has been largely abandoned. They are very affectionate dogs, enjoy life in a human family, follow their owners obediently, wish to please, and are intelligent and eager learners as they enjoy being trained.

They are often taken to competitions and seem to enjoy tests of agility, obedience, tracking, and herding. A fit Corgi can run at speeds of up to twenty-five miles per hour in spite of its short legs.

Corgis rank high for friendliness with family, kids, and strangers. They are very intelligent and easy to train but they do bark at times. Additionally, Corgis are energetic, playful, have a big appetite, and love lots of exercise.

There are two types of Corgi, the Pembroke Welsh Corgi and the Cardigan Welsh Corgi, which is slightly larger and has a long tail. Pembroke Corgis are usually redheads, while the Cardigan Corgis can be red, sable, black, tan, brindle, or blue merle.

CORGI CROWN

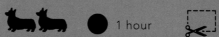 1 hour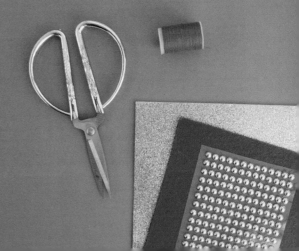

Holly the Corgi always carries herself with style and now with her new crown she has an extra bounce in her step! A fun accessory for any "top dog," Holly is going places.

Some snipping and a few quick stitches will result in a gorgeous little crown fit for any dog. You can also make your crown with glue for a no-sew option. What do you say, Holly?

YOU WILL NEED:

- Felt
- Scissors
- Glitter foam sheet
- Sticky gems
- Needle and thread

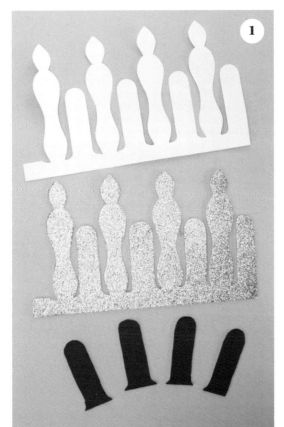

HOW TO MAKE
YOUR CROWN:

1.

Copy the template in this book and cut your crown template out of foam sheet or felt.

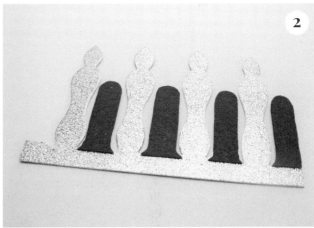

2.

Place the red felt panels on the crown and secure in place with fabric glue.

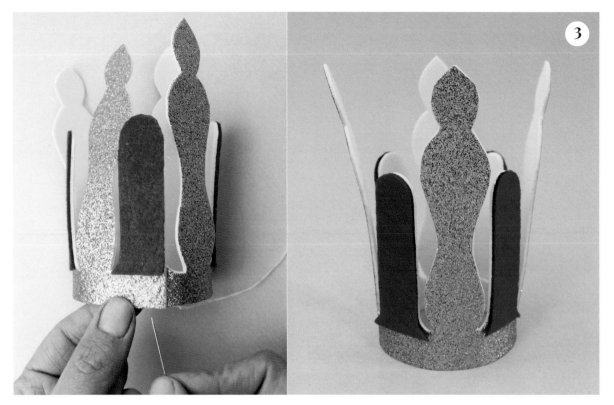

3. Make a cross stitch to join the tabs together and make the circular crown.

4. Next take the shorter middle tabs and join them together with a stitch.

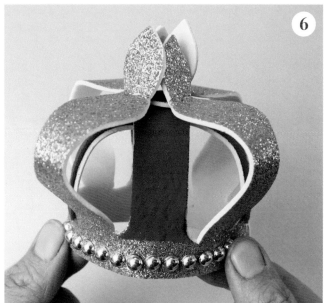

5. Now fold in the top tabs and add a stitch at the base of each leaf shape.

6. Add some optional jewels and your crown is ready.

7. We used a ribbon on each side to attach the crown to Holly the Corgi's head.

Corgis Rule

CORGI HOODIE

 1–2 hours

How about a cozy Corgi hoodie? All you'll need is a fleecy hoodie to up-cycle into this adorable DIY Corgi outfit. Perfect for snuggling up on the sofa or taking a walk around the block.

Make your own Corgi kigurumi in no time by following these simple steps. It's a dog's life!

YOU WILL NEED:

- Hooded top
- Scissors
- Cushion filling
- Felt in various colors
  (brown, black, yellow, pink, and white)
- Cream fleecy fabric
- Needle and thread

HOW TO MAKE YOUR HOODIE:

1. Use the templates in this book, or draw your own Corgi face, ears, and paws. Cut out the templates.

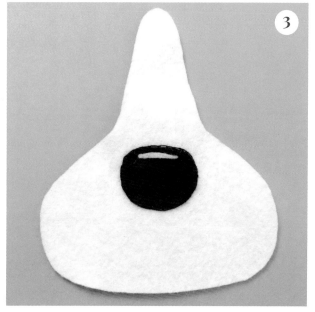

2. Next, cut out the eyes, nose, and mouth from felt or scraps of fabric.

3. Use a blanket stitch to attach the nose to the white panel as shown.

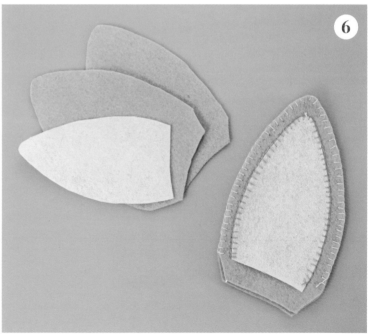

4. Add a little cushion stuffing inside.

5. Next, add your Corgi eyes and eyebrows.

6. Now to prepare those ears! Sew two panels of orange felt together and add a paler panel.

7.

Sew the ears in place on the
back of the hood as shown.

8.

Add an optional pink felt tongue.

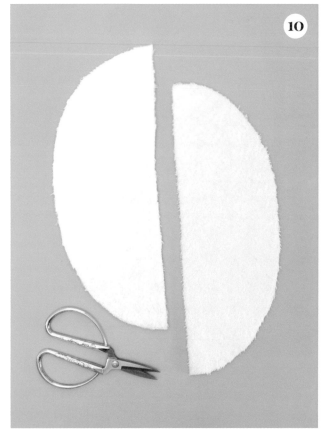

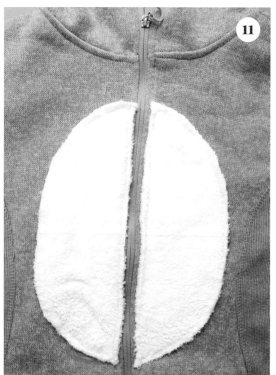

9. Stitch the paws in place on the inner cuffs.

10. Cut out two panels of pale or white fleece.

11. Carefully stitch in place on the front of your top.

12.

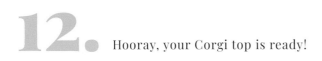

Hooray, your Corgi top is ready!

CORGI PLANTER

  2 hours *Plus drying time

Make an adorable Corgi planter using air- or oven-dry clay.
Mold a ball of clay into a sitting Corgi, then pack with earth and
mini succulents for a unique planter!

Paint on a happy face and little pink paws.

YOU WILL NEED:

- Clay (air or oven dry)
- Modeling tools
- Acrylic paint
- Succulents

HOW TO MAKE
YOUR PLANTER:

1. Break off a handful of clay and form a ball. Scoop out the center.

2. Using your thumbs, smooth out a deep well in the center of the ball.

3. Take two small balls of clay and model them to make the front legs.

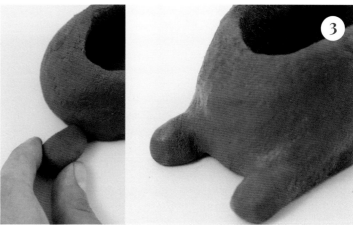

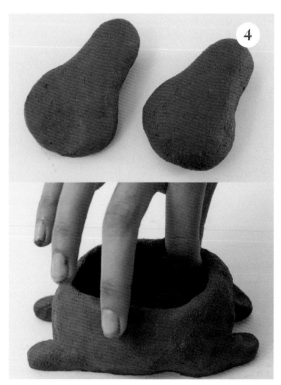

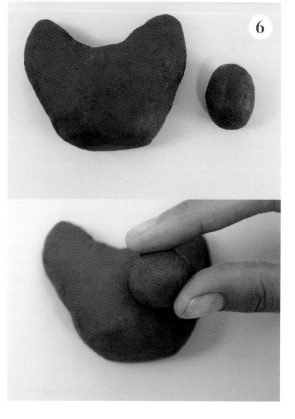

4. Use larger pieces to make the back legs and attach to the main planter, smoothing the clay.

5. Next, take a smaller ball to make the Corgi head. Form two ear-shaped pieces of clay.

6. Add another ball to form the nose. Smooth in place.

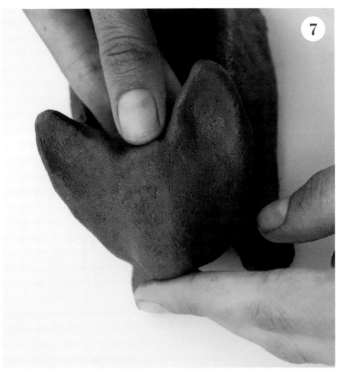

7.

Attach the head to the
planter body as shown.

8.

Add a small tail to the
back and smooth in place.

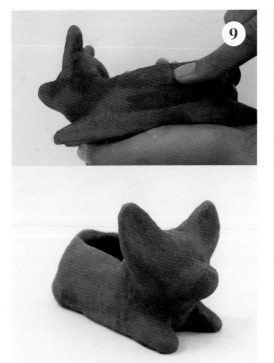

9.

Take some water and smooth out the planter with your finger or a sponge.

10.

Once your planter is fully dry, add white paint as shown. Use the natural color of the clay as brown areas of the Corgi's hair.

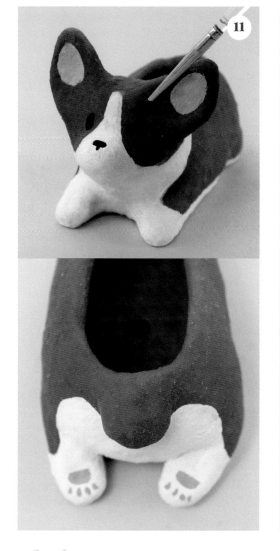

11. Paint eyes, nose, ears, and paws. Add a coat of varnish to the white areas and inside.

12. Once the paint and varnish is fully dry, fill your planter with dirt.

13. Add a selection of succulents and your planter is ready!

TIP!

Use the end of a paint brush to make a small hole in the base of your planter.

CORGI CRAFTS

CORGI BROOCH

 ●● 2 hours ✂

Make a needle felt brooch, full of Corgi character!
Sculpt unspun wool, using special needles to lock the fibers of
wool together. Once you get to grips with the technique it is very
satisfying and you can create wonderful characters in no time.

Model your brooch on your own pet or favorite Corgi.
This project is not for younger crafters to tackle alone
as the needles are very sharp, so please take care!

YOU WILL NEED:

- Unspun wool in various colors
- Foam pad
- Felting needles
- Scissors
- Brooch pin
- Eye studs (optional)

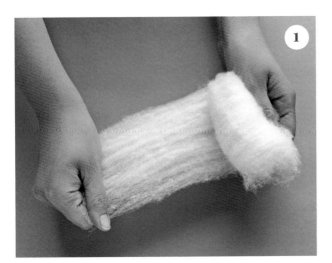

HOW TO MAKE
YOUR BROOCH:

1.

Separate around 11g of raw wool you
need to make your brooch.

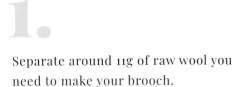

2.

Separate a length of wool and tear it in
to four equal pieces. Lay them on top
of each other with the wool lying in
opposite directions.

3.

Take a felting needle and a sponge. Form an oval by poking the wool repeatedly with the needle. Use the chart at the back of this book to hold to the correct size.

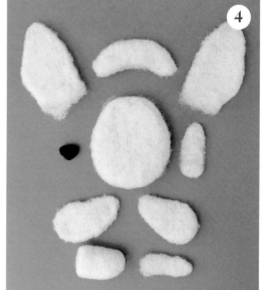

4.

Repeat these steps to form the ears, forehead, snout, and mouth.

5.

Now to start building the form of your Corgi face. Use the needle to attach the pieces of the face to the base.

6.

Next, fold a piece of black felt in the shape of the nose and attach to the face using the needle.

7.

Then add the eyes. You can use eye studs from the craft store or fashion them out of black wool.

8.

Now to add some ochre or light brown wool. Start by holding around the top of the ears, then move on to the top of the face as shown. Next add another layer of white wool to the face.

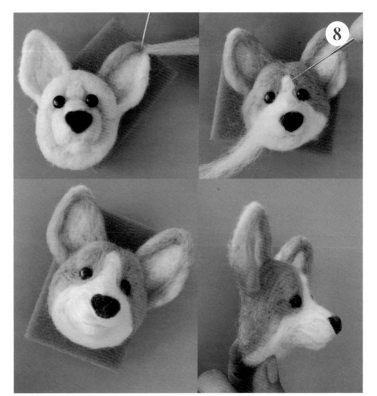

9.

Cut a tongue from pink felt and use the needle to poke it in place. Run a thin line of black wool around the bottom of the snout to form the mouth.

10.

Now to add a ruff around the neck. Build up layers of white wool in the center and add more ochre wool around the sides. Poke them in place at the top only, so that they fall free, like hair.

11.

Trim the ruff to the desired length as shown.

12.

How about a bandana?
Cut off a scrap of material
and use the needle to poke
the corners in place.

13.

Now it is time to add the brooch pin.
You can do this using the wool, too!
Work a large piece up and down the
back of the pin poking it in to place.
Finally, form a circular piece to finish
off the back of the brooch.

CORGI ROCK PAINTING

 ● 1 hour

Rock painting is an unique and easy craft with fun results!
All you'll need is a couple of smooth stones or rocks from
your garden, local park, or beach.

Pick smooth, flat rocks, as it's harder to decorate ones with ridges.
If you can't find them in nature, check out your local craft store.

Next, choose an image for your rock. You could be inspired by your
own pet, a favorite photo, or your imagination. Sketch out your
idea and off you go! You can give painted rocks as gifts,
use them to decorate your garden, or use them as paperweights.

YOU WILL NEED:

- Selection of rocks (smooth and flat)
- Acrylic paint
- Acrylic varnish
- Paint brushes

HOW TO PAINT YOUR ROCK:

1.

Select nice flat rocks for painting. Wash the rocks before decorating them.

2.

Prime with white paint to help the colors that you paint on top appear more vibrant.

3. Sketch out your design, then use a pencil to transfer your design to the rock surface. A rough outline is fine as a guide.

4. Add your first coat of colored paint and let it dry.

5. Next, add details—here we added the tongue and the butterfly.

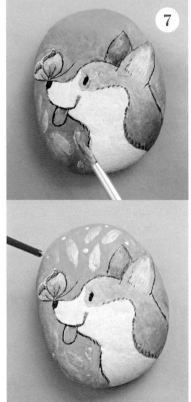

6.

Build up the layers of your design. Once your background color is dry, use a pen or small brush to add the finer details.

7.

Then add leaves and foliage. We used metallic paint to add some shine. Turn your paint brush around and use the tip to add neat dots of color.

8.

Once the paint is dry, add a coat of acrylic varnish. This will protect your painted rocks from the elements.

CORGI MUG

 ● 1 hour ✂️ ⬚

Make your own special mug for tea time! This is an easy project and makes a great gift. Pick up some ceramic markers at your local craft store and get creative.

Add a message to your mug or the name of your favorite Corgi! Add a Corgi smile on the bottom of your mug and you'll have everyone else smiling, too!

YOU WILL NEED:

- White mug
- Ceramic markers
- Ceramic paint
- Pencils and paper
- Ballpoint pen
- Scissors
- Masking tape

HOW TO MAKE YOUR MUG:

1.

Clean your mug and draw out your design, or use the templates in the back of this book. Remember to add a little width to the Corgi face as it will appear narrower on the curve of the mug.

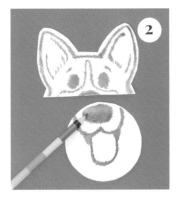

2.

Once you are happy with your design, use a soft pencil to scribble on the reverse of your design.

3.

Tape your designs in position on your mug.

4.

Next, use a ballpoint pen and go over the design.

5. This will create a guide in pencil on your mug surface.

6. Now break out the colors. We started with an ochre ceramic paint and to fill out the Corgi face. You could also use a ceramic marker.

7. Add details with ceramic markers. Carefully outline the image with black or dark brown.

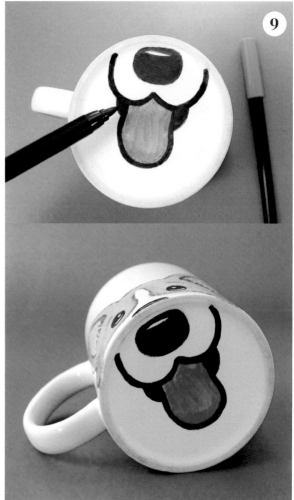

8. Add some color to your design.

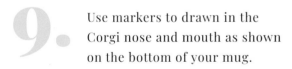
9. Use markers to drawn in the Corgi nose and mouth as shown on the bottom of your mug.

10.

Next, add a message on the other side of the mug—*"I'm all ears!"* You could also add the name of your dog or another message.

11.

Place your mug upside down on a baking tray. Follow the directions on the markers you are using. We baked our mug in the oven for 25 minutes on a medium heat.

CORGI MAGNETS

 1 hour

Magnets are so fun and easy to make, and useful, too! We couldn't resist making a cute Corgi face and classic Corgi fluffy butt combo. This craft doesn't take long and you can make as many different magnets as you like. Why not try out some different Corgi poses?

Once they're ready, use them on your fridge or notice board to keep on top of things!

YOU WILL NEED:

- Modeling clay
- Modeling tools
- Magnets
- Acrylic paint
- Glue

HOW TO MAKE YOUR MAGNETS:

1.

Take a piece of clay (approximately 1½ inches in diameter) and roll it in to a ball.

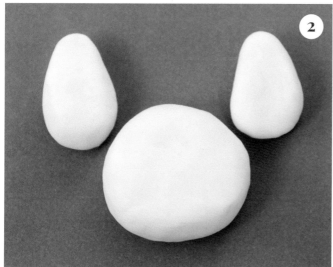

2.

Flatten the ball and use more clay to make two ear shapes as shown.

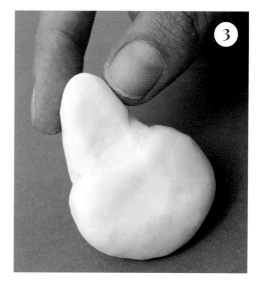

3.

Attach the ears to the ball...

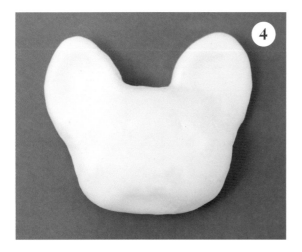

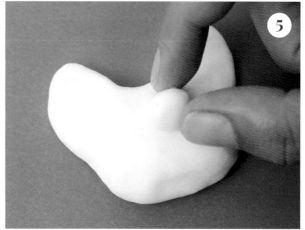

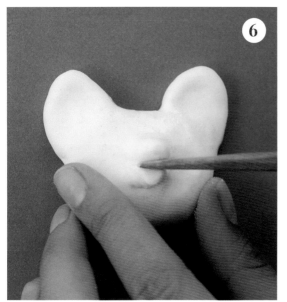

4. . . . and smooth into place.

5. Add a small ball as the Corgi's nose.

6. Take a modeling tool or knife and make a dent at the bottom of the nose to form the mouth.

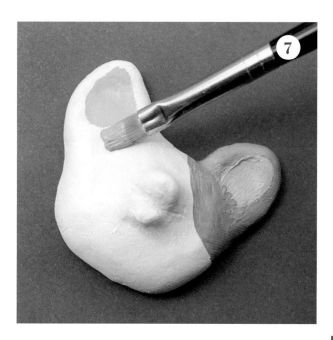

56

7.

Now to start painting. Start with a base coat of white, then add coloring and ears.

8.

Now carefully add pink tongue, plus eyes, nose, and mouth. Set your Corgi to one side to dry.

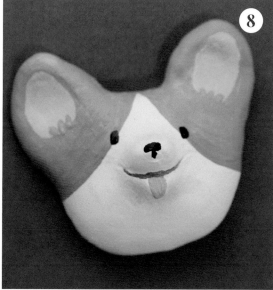

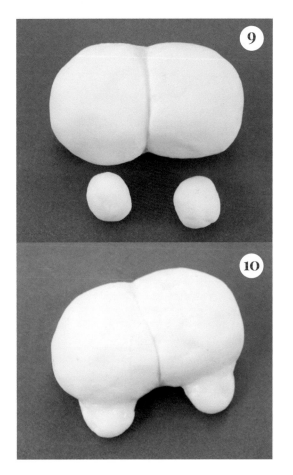

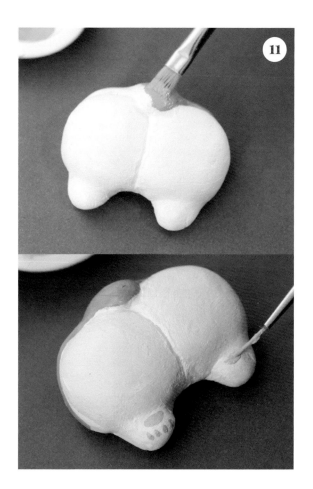

9.

Now to make a Corgi butt!
Take two small balls of clay, around
¾ inch in diameter each. Merge them
together to make a fluffy butt.

10.

Break off two smaller
balls to form the feet
and attach as shown.

11.

Paint tan fur and little
pink paws in place.

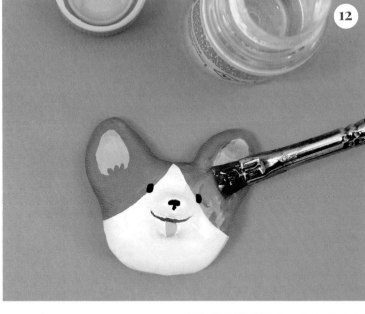

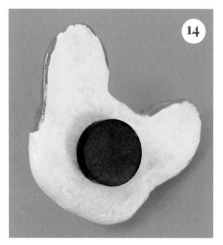

12.

Add a coat of varnish to your Corgi face and butt.

13.

Once the varnish is dry, you can attach the magnets.

14.

Stick the magnets to the reverse of your clay using strong liquid glue or a glue gun.

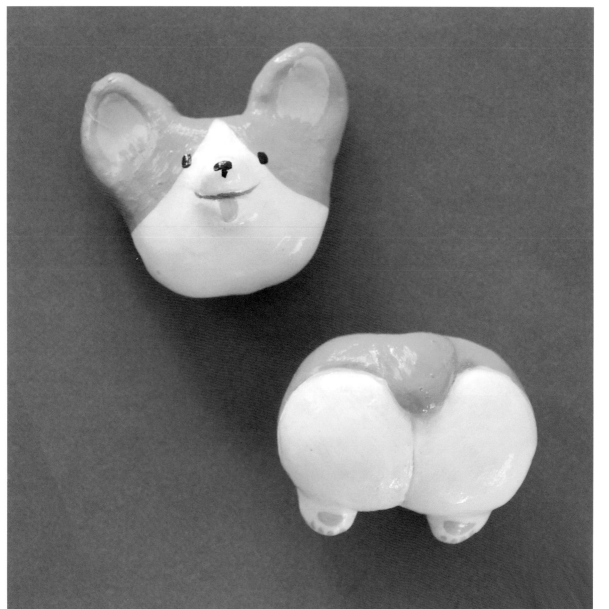

CORGI HAT

 ● 1 hour ✂

Brave the cold with this cute and cozy fleecy hat.
Choose your favorite Corgi tones, or match to your own dog.

The steps are so simple, so grab some fleece (or recycle
an old top) and you'll be rocking the Corgi style in no time!

YOU WILL NEED:

- Fleece material in light
  brown and cream or white
- Black and white felt
- Needle and thread

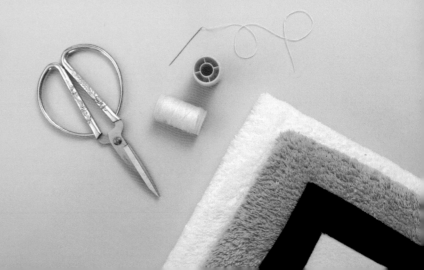

HOW TO MAKE YOUR HAT:

1. Copy and cut out the template in this book or draw your own.

2. Stick the pieces of the template together as shown.

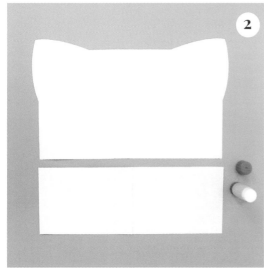

3. Draw around templates 1&2 onto the brown fleece.

4. Carefully cut two copies of each hat template out of the fleece.

5. Sew each section together, back-to-back, as shown.

6. Turn the top section of the hat around, so the stitching is on the inside.

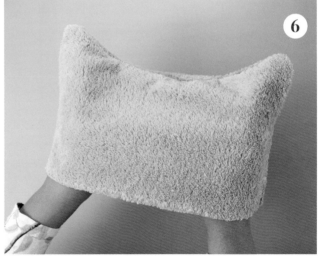

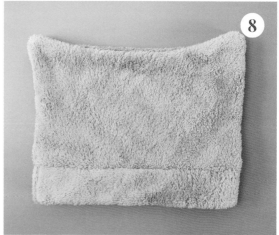

7. Now take the hat band and double it over, folding it in half lengthwise. Take the raw edges and sew them to the raw edge of the top of the hat, then flip down.

8. The main part of your hat is ready!

9. Stitch around the top of the ears as shown, to add detail.

10.

Now stitch the cream fleece nose panel onto your hat. Cut out the nose panel from cream fleece and the eyes and nose from black felt. Add white felt highlights.

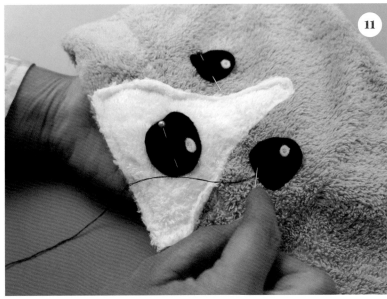

11.

Pin the eyes and nose in place and stitch in place as shown.

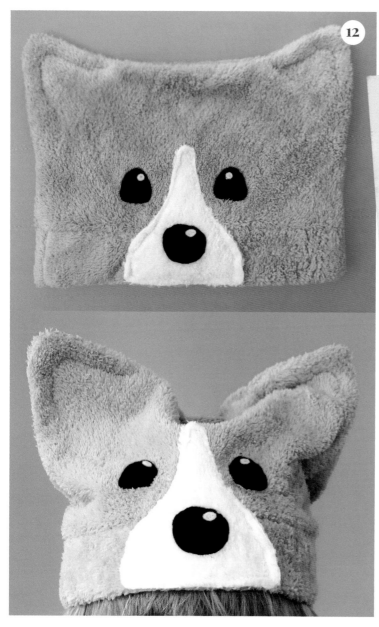

Ivan and Holly

12.

Your hat is ready. Pop it on your head to see the Corgi ears in all their glory!

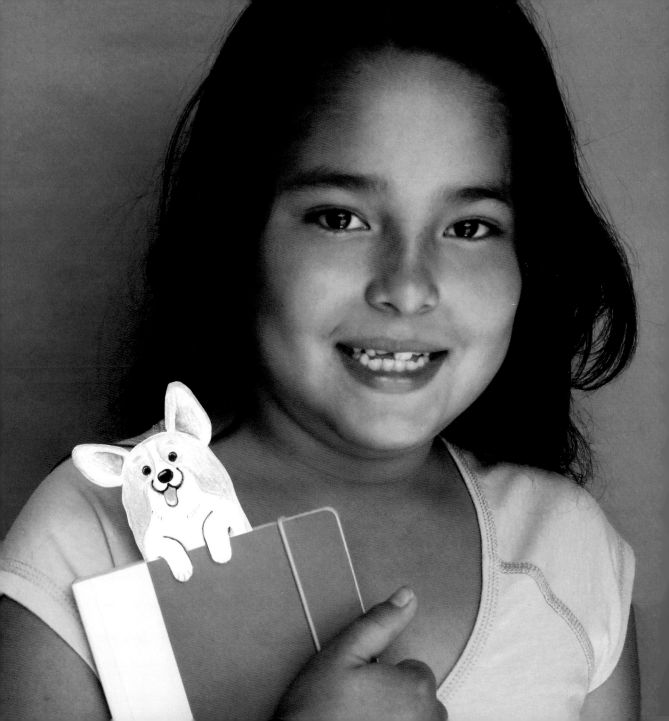

CORGI BOOKMARK

 ● 1 hour ✂

Use the template in this book to make your very own Corgi bookmark. What could be cuter than a friendly Corgi peeping over the top of your book, keeping your place?

All you need for this easy craft is card stock, colors, and glue. Color in your Corgi any way you choose. So let's get started!

YOU WILL NEED:

- Scissors
- White card stock
- Colored pencils
- Glue stick
- Craft knife

HOW TO MAKE YOUR BOOKMARK:

1.

Copy the bookmark template at the back of the book, or draw your own.

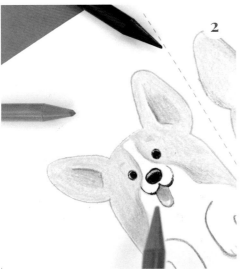

2.
Next, color in the template, front and back.

3.
Using a craft knife, carefully cut around the Corgi paws.

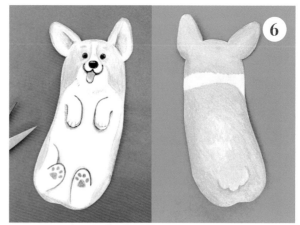

4. Next, fold the template in half along the dotted line.

5. Glue the panels back to back, avoiding the paw area.

6. Carefully cut out your Corgi bookmark and check front and back.

7. Make as many Corgi bookmarks as you like, with different color ways and expressions.

CORGI STRING ART

 ●● 2 hours

String art is a creative way to make a colorful picture, by wrapping thread around nails. Mix up the colors and have fun creating unique piece of artwork. Give little ones a hand by putting nails in place, then they can have fun wrapping around the colorful thread.

YOU WILL NEED:

- Wooden board
- Small nails
- Hammer
- Pliers
- Colorful embroidery threads or fine string
- Acrylic paints

HOW TO MAKE YOUR STRING ART:

1.

Choose a board of wood and scale your template to fit.

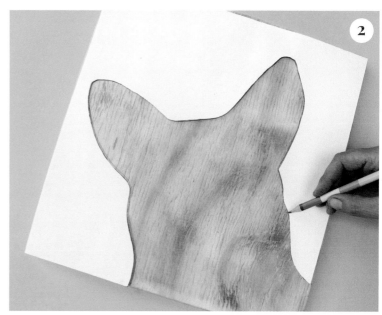

2.

Cut out the center of your Corgi head as shown and trace around the line.

3.

Now to paint the base coat. Use white paint as a base for your Corgi head and add a colorful background.

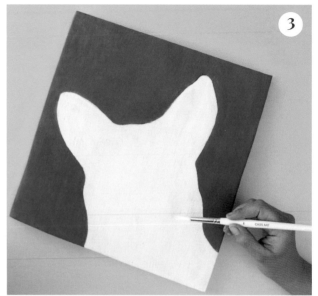

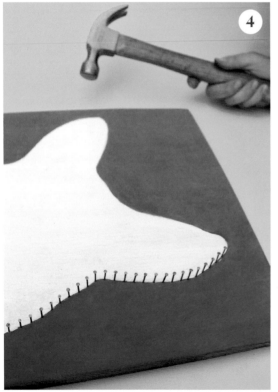

4.

Following the line, nail in small nails, at approximately ⅒ of an inch intervals.

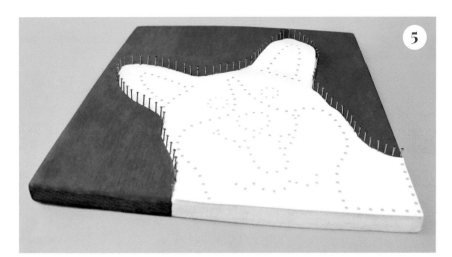

5.

Place your Corgi face template inside the nails as shown.

6.

Following the guide, add the rest of the nails. It helps to use pliers to hold the nails in place.

7.

Once you have completed the design, tear off the paper reference.

8.

Start by wrapping a length of thread around the first nail, tying a knot to secure it.

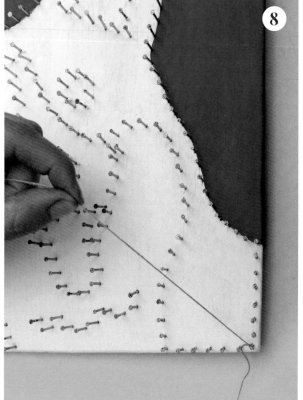

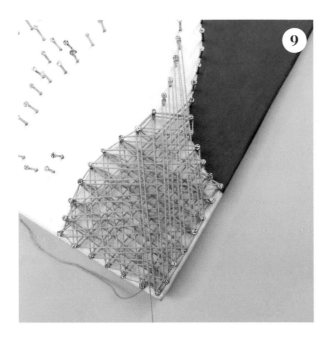

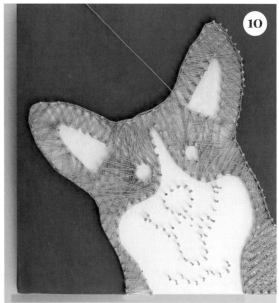

9.

Start wrapping the thread between each nail until the space is filled. You can wrap the string in any direction—make a random pattern or follow a grid. There are no rules!

10.

Carry on wrapping until the light brown areas are covered.

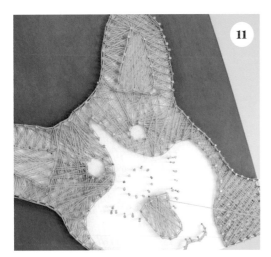

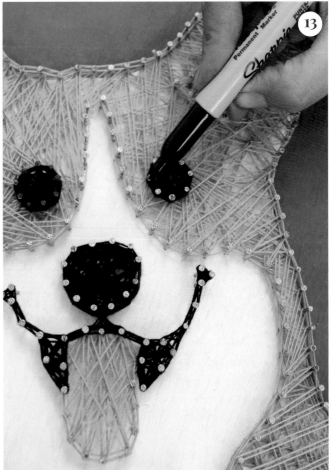

11. Now add pink thread for the tongue and ears.

12. Use black thread for the mouth, nose, and eyes.

13. Lastly take a black Sharpie and color in the top of the nails for the eyes, mouth, and nose.

CORGI CUSHION

1 hour

This Corgi cushion will look lovely nestled on your sofa or bed.
Choose a colorful patterned fabric for the top section,
or recycle a pretty T-shirt or pillow case.

You can fill your Corgi cushion with stuffing or with recycled
scrap fabric. Why not make a whole family of Corgis, in
different colors and patterns?

YOU WILL NEED:

- Scissors
- Needle and thread
- Cushion stuffing
- Cream or white fabric
- Colorful patterned fabric

HOW TO MAKE
YOUR CUSHION:

1.

Copy and cut out the Corgi
cushion templates in this book,
or draw your own.

2.

Trace the Corgi pattern on to
your base cream or white fabric.
Add a margin of ¼ inch.

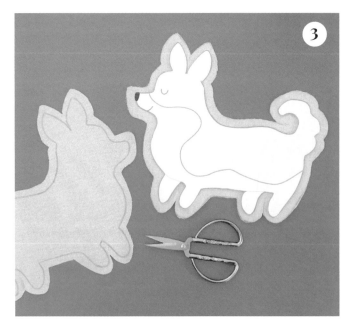

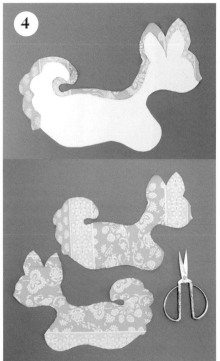

3. Cut out two Corgi templates from the fabric as shown.

4. Now cut out two copies of your patterned fabric.

5. Sew the colored panels on to your cushion base templates.

6.

Sew a chain stitch mouth and eye on each side of your Corgi cushion using black thread.

7.

Sew the two panels together, back to back, leaving a gap at the bottom of the Corgi body. Trim away the excess material.

8.

Carefully turn the cushion the right way round. Use a paint brush or similar to poke in to the legs and nose to turn them around.

9.

Fill the Corgi with cushion stuffing.

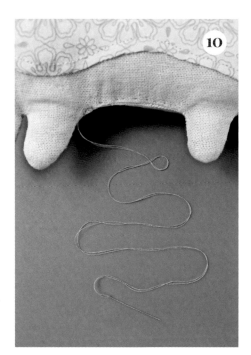

10.

Sew up the bottom panel.

11.

Add the nose, stitching black thread around the front of the two panels.

12.

Your gorgeous Corgi cushion is ready!

CORGI EYE MASK

 ● 1 hour ✂

Sleep easy with an adorable DIY Corgi eye mask. Blocking out light helps to promote healthy sleep patterns. It's much easier to fall asleep on a bright train, bus, or plane when you can pull a soft, cozy mask over your eyes to block out the world and drift off.

This cute mask even has flappy Corgi ears and is surprisingly easy to make. Perfect as a gift for the Corgi lover in your life, especially if that happens to be you!

YOU WILL NEED:

- Soft velour material (orange and white)
- Black felt material
- Elastic band (¼ inch wide)
- Scissors and pins
- Needle and thread

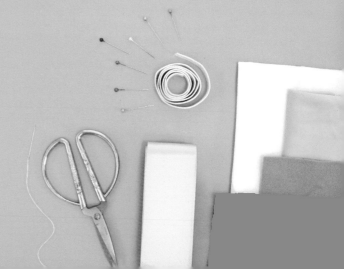

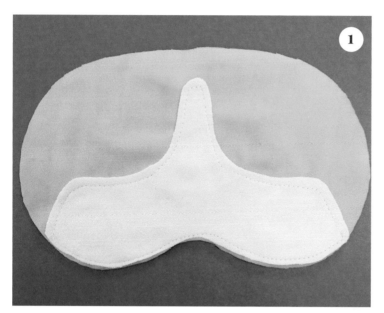

HOW TO MAKE YOUR EYE MASK:

1.

Using the templates in this book, cut out the templates for your mask. Sew the white panel in position on the base.

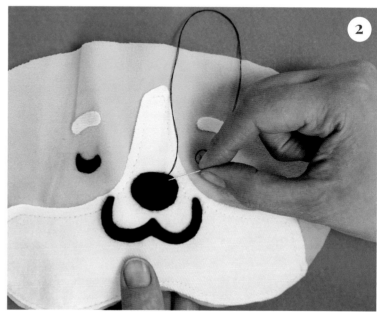

2.

Next add the eyes, nose, mouth, and eyebrows.

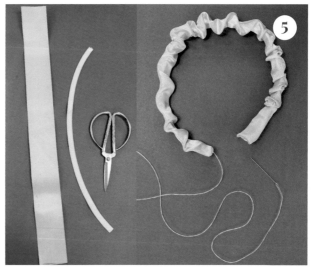

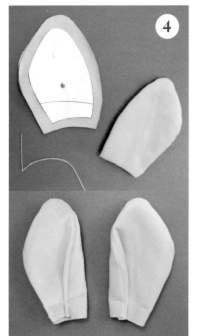

3. Add a pink tongue, just stitching it to the mouth along the top edge.

4. Stitch two templates back to back for each ear. Turn the ears the right way around then stitch in place a small fold on the inner edge as shown.

5. Double over the length of ribbon, then sew the length of elastic inside.

6.

Now to assemble your mask. Place the ears in position, then fold them forward so that they will be in position once your mask is sewn together.

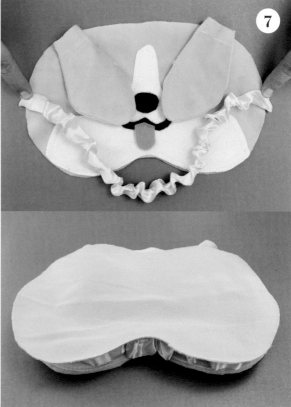

7.

Pin the head band in place on either side of the mask. Finally place the second mask panel face down on top, making sure that the ears and band are tucked inside. Loosely pin the sides together.

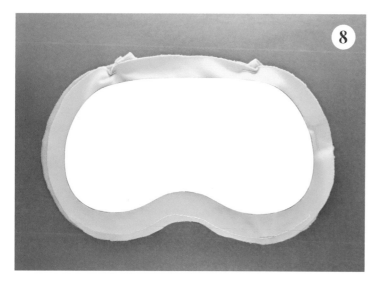

8.

Using the template as a guide, carefully stitch around the outer line, joining the two sides of the mask together. Leave a small hole at the top of the mask so that you can turn it around the right way.

9.

Make a small cut at the base of the mask as shown. This will make it easier to turn the mask the right way around.

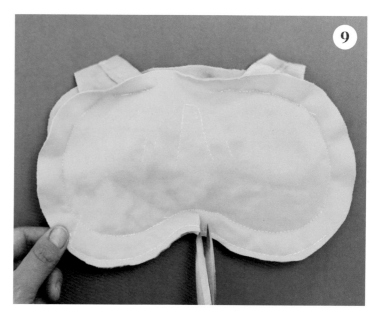

10.

Carefully turn your Corgi mask around the right way and check that everything is in the right place.

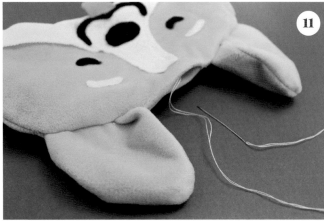

11.

Finally, sew up the hole at the top of the mask. Hooray, your Corgi eye mask is ready! Time for a snooze.

TIP!

Create your bracelet using your own color combination.

CORGI BEAD BRACELET

  2 hours

Wear a Corgi on your wrist with this loom-woven beadwork bracelet. Weave the pattern by inserting the weft threads (side to side threads) over and under the stationary warp threads (up and down threads).

The warp threads are held in place by tension, and the weft threads, which hold your beads, are woven between them.

Besides a bead loom, you'll also need seed beads, thread, and needles.

YOU WILL NEED:

- A bead loom
- Colorful seed beads
- Beading thread
- Beading needles
- Scissors

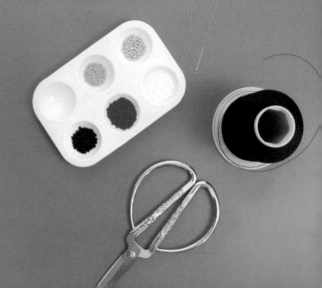

HOW TO MAKE
YOUR BRACELET:

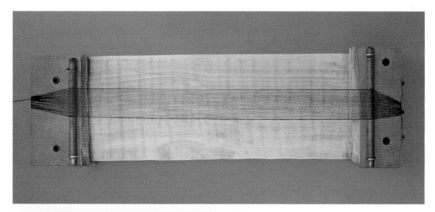

For this project you will need a bead loom. You can use a DIY loom or buy one from your local craft store or online supplier.

1.

Set up the warp threads (those that are attached to the loom). The design featured in this book is 22 beads high, so you'll need 23 warp threads. Cut 23 lengths of thread of about 40 inches long, and knot them together at one end in a loop. Hook the loop onto the nail head at one end of the loom, then tie the threads to a nail at the other end. Separate each of the threads evenly.

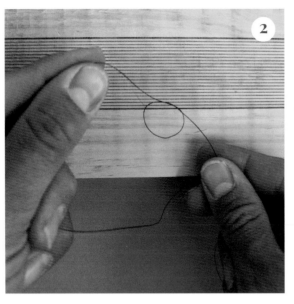

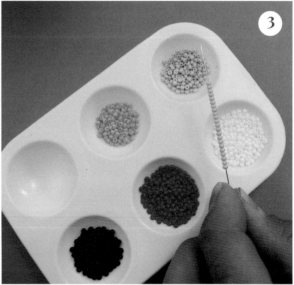

2. Tie a long piece of thread on to the bottom warp thread as shown, so that your design will sit in roughly the middle of the loom. Ideally you don't want to have to change your thread, so cut a piece of thread that is long, but manageable.

3. Add a needle to the end of your thread and then thread your first row of 22 beads and keep them on the needle without moving them down the thread. Follow the pattern on the template. For example, row 1 has 22 blue beads.

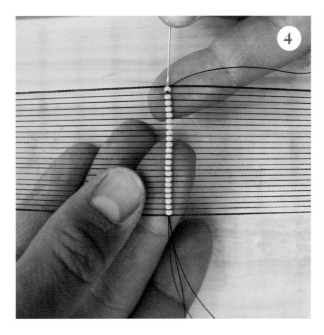

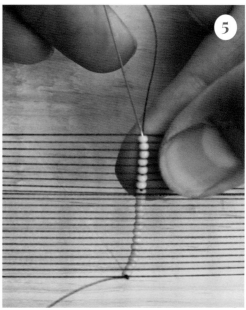

4. Lay the needle on top of the warp threads and arrange the beads so that they sit between the threads as shown. Use your finger to hold the beads in place and pull the needle through. Leave a length of thread hanging from the front bead.

5. Turn your needle around and thread back through the beads. This time, make sure the needle goes underneath each of the warp threads as you pass it through the holes in the beads.

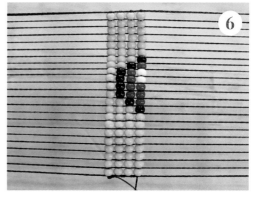

6. Count the order of beads on the template to create the image.

7.

For example, row two has 10 blue beads, followed by 4 black beads, followed by 8 blue beads. Load these beads on to your needle and repeat the steps.

8.

Once you have completed the rows to create your image, it is time to finish each side of the bracelet.

9.

Add one less bead to the needle to decrease the number of beads in each row as shown.

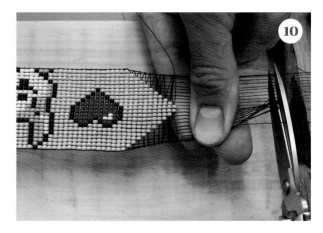

10.

When this is done cut the warp threads loose from the loom. Leave plenty of length.

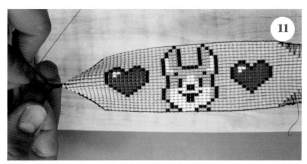

11.

Remove the needle and add the thread to the warp threads. Separate the threads into three groups and braid them.

12.

Add a secure knot at the end and trim any excess.

13.

Attach a tassel to the each side and you're ready to wear your bracelet! Secure it with a double knot.

CORGI PLATES

 ● 1 hour ✂

This decoupage technique is suprisingly easy and gives great results. Use a patterned paper napkin to add a vibrant background or paint a bright color behind your image.

Pick up some glass plates at your local hardware store and get creative. Display your plates on a dresser or fill a wall with plates for maximum impact!

YOU WILL NEED:

- Glass plates
- Mod Podge or white glue
- Paper napkins
- Paint brush or sponge
- Acrylic paints
- Scissors

HOW TO MAKE YOUR PLATES:

1.

First, pick out your design. Use a photo or illustration. Scan in and print out, or laser copy. Make a quick test first to be sure that your printout doesn't smudge.

2.

Assemble your design. Using the templates in this book, add accessories with a glue stick. Looking smart!

3. Add coat of Mod Podge or white glue to the reverse of your clean glass paint.

4. Carefully place your paper design face down. Add a little more glue and brush in to place. Allow to dry.

5. Take a patterned paper napkin and remove the plain layers of napkin and just use the patterned layer.

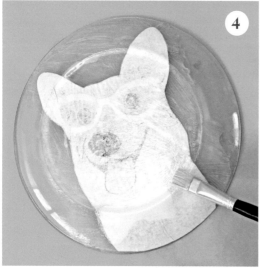

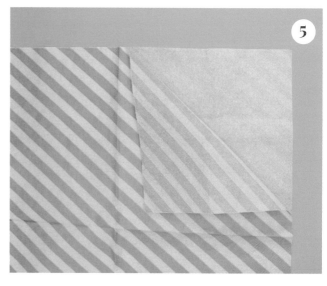

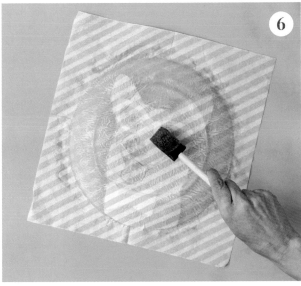

6. Place the napkin face down on the reverse of the plate, "behind" your design. Starting from the center, carefully secure it in place using a sponge as shown.

7. Leave your plate to fully dry. Once it is dry trim roughly around the edges.

8. Use a nail file to remove the excess napkin, sweeping from back to front. Add a coat of white acrylic to the back of the plate.

TIP!

As an easy alternative to paper napkins, paint the reverse of your plate with a bright color.

CORGI
PLUSH

 ● ● 2 hours ✂

Make your own cuddly Corgi plush!
This happy Corgi plush is full of character. Follow
the pattern in this book to make your Corgi friend.

Add a colorful bandana as a finishing touch.
Great as a gift for any Corgi lover!

YOU WILL NEED:

- Felt in yellow, orange, white, and pink
- Scissors
- Needle and thread
- Cushion stuffing

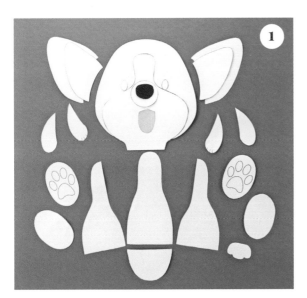

HOW TO MAKE YOUR PLUSH:

1.

Copy and cut out the plush templates at the back of this book.

2.

Cut out the templates for the Corgi head and ears.

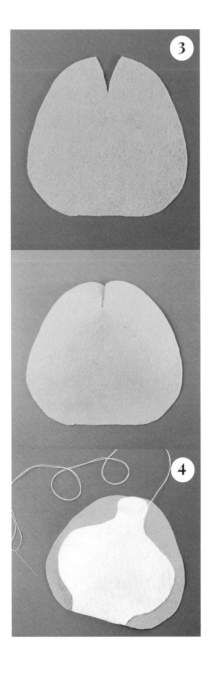

3. Sew together the gap at the top of panel 1.

4. Stitch the white panel on to the front of panel 1. We used a blanket stitch.

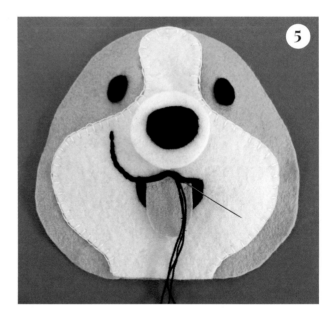

5. Cut out the facial features in felt and attach to the face as shown, using needle and thread. Sew the Corgi's smile in place using a chain stitch.

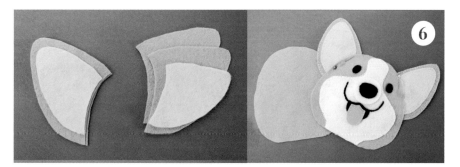

6.

Sew the ears in place, then connect the two head panels using a blanket stitch. Leave the neck open.

7.

Stuff your Corgi head with cushion filling as shown.

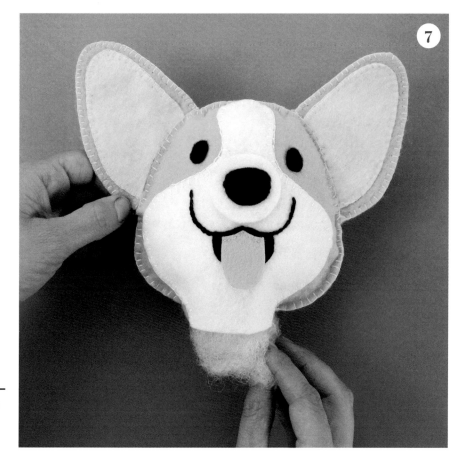

8.

Now take the body and feet panels.

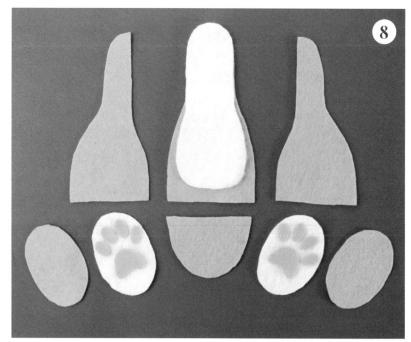

9.

Connect the two body panels as shown.

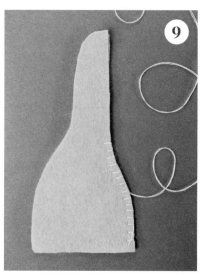

10.

Add the white front piece to the third body panel.

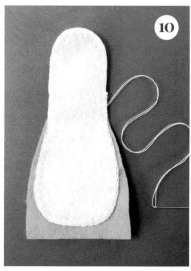

11.

Connect the three panels and stuff them with cushion filling.

12.

Seal the body with the triangular panel at the base.

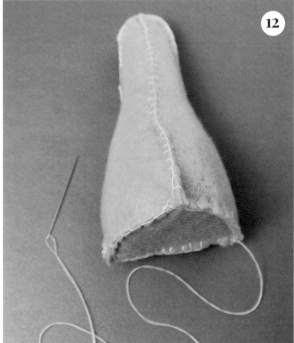

13.

Now sew together and
fill the arms and paws.

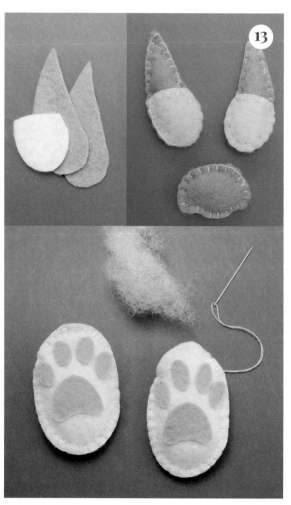

14.

Using thread, attach them
to the Corgi body.

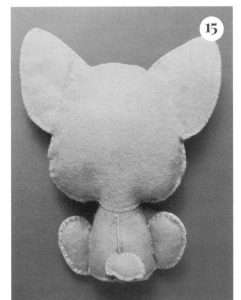

15.

Then attach the front and back of the head to the body. Add the tail to the reverse.

16.

Finish off your Corgi plush with a tiny colorful bandana!

CORGI GIFT BOXES

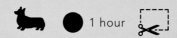 ● 1 hour ✂

These cute little boxes are perfect for filling with special gifts for fellow Corgi lovers. Make the boxes any size you need by adjusting the size of the template.

These neat boxes are perfect as favors for your next party too. Fill them with candy or small treats.

YOU WILL NEED:

- Brown, yellow, and orange card stock
- White paper
- Scissors
- Glue stick
- Pens and pencils

HOW TO MAKE YOUR BOXES:

1.

Copy and trace the templates in this book, or use your own.

2.

Carefully cut out the templates.

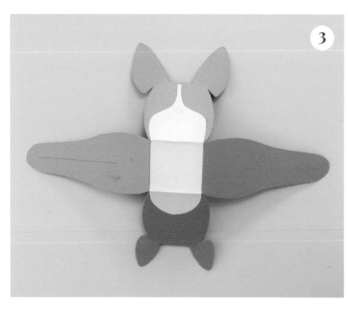

3.

Score and fold the box template where indicated and stick the white panel in place using a glue stick.

4.

Using a craft knife, cut two slits as shown.

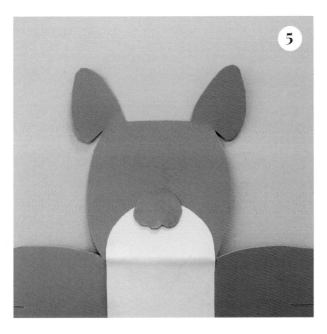

Place a fluffy or longer tail on the reverse of the box.

5.

Take a pen and draw the eyes, nose, and mouth in place.

6.

Cut out a pink paper tongue and glue in place.

7.

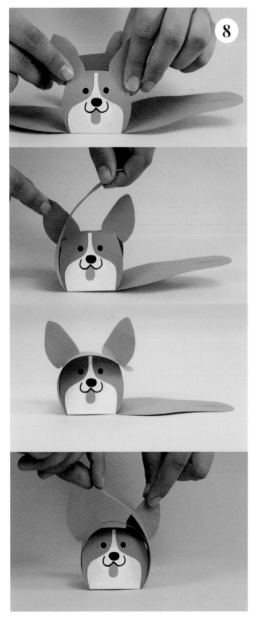

8. To close your gift box, pinch together the ears and pull one tab over both ears so they slip through the slot. Pull the other tab over both ears to close.

9. Your Corgi gift box is ready!

CORGI NECKLACE

 ● 1 hour

Follow these simple steps, make and bake your Corgi charm, then paint it your way. Attach to a jewelry chain and you are ready to go. Add a tassel too for a splash of color.

These adorable charm necklaces make great gifts for any Corgi lover in your life!

YOU WILL NEED:

- Porcelain or polymer clay
- Jewelry chain and clasps
- Acrylic paint
- Acrylic varnish
- Modeling tools

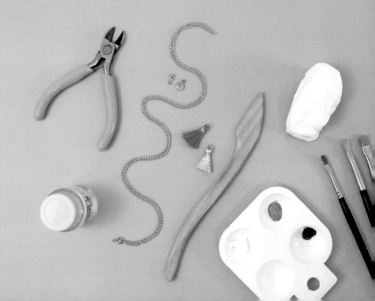

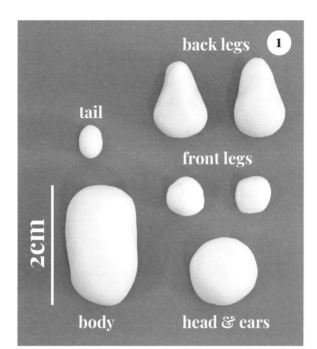

tail

back legs

front legs

2cm

body

head & ears

HOW TO MAKE YOUR NECKLACE:

1.

First assemble the pieces of clay you will need for your Corgi necklace: an egg shape for the body, two back legs, two smaller front legs, a tail, and a head.

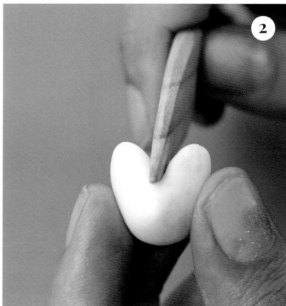

2.

Take your clay head and mold the ears of your Corgi. You can use a tool or your fingers.

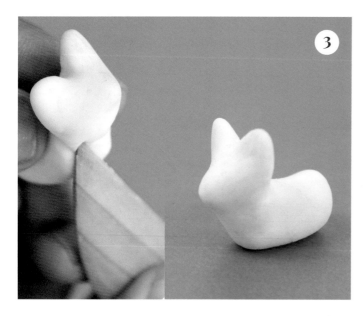

3.

Next, attach the head
to the body as shown.

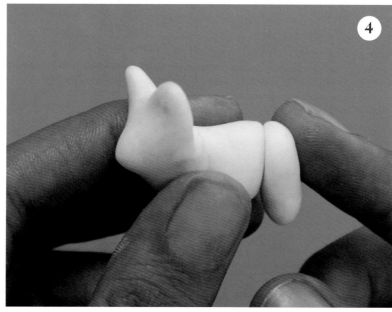

4.

Carefully attach the
larger back legs.

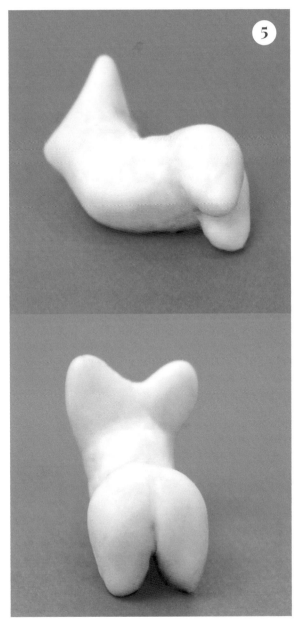

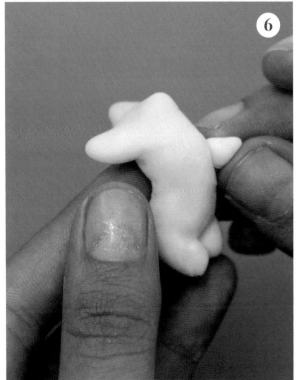

5. Smooth over to create your Corgi butt!

6. Now carefully add the front legs.

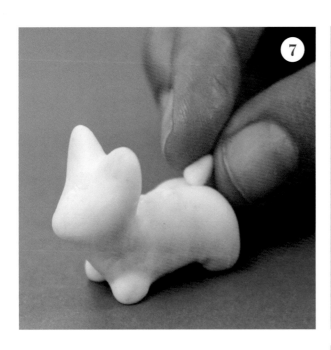

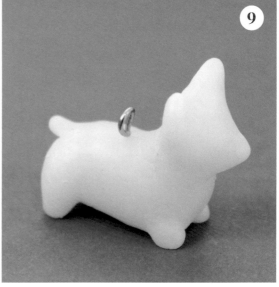

7. Lastly add the Corgi's tail.

8. Why not make a few Corgis to decorate with different colors?

9. Add a small jewelers hoop to the back of each Corgi.

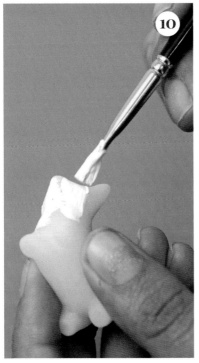

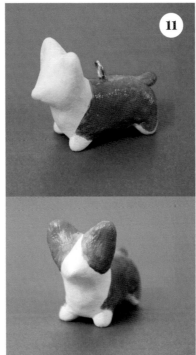

10.

Once your clay is dry (or baked if needed) you can start painting. Start with a base coat of white.

11.

Next add the Corgi's coloring.

12.

Carefully add the eyes and nose.

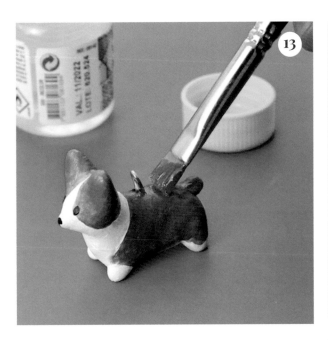

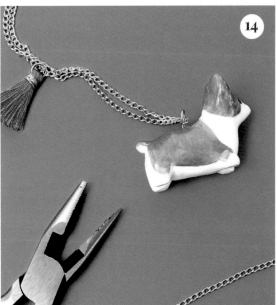

Once the paint is dry, add a coat of acrylic varnish.

13.

Attach a chain of your choice.

14.

Cut the chain to the length of your choice using pliers and add a clasp.

15.

NOT TODAY..

LET'S GO!

CORGI DOOR HANGER

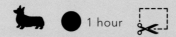 ● 1 hour ✂️

Knock, knock! Make your own Corgi door hanger.

Could there be a cuter way to tell the world you're taking it easy, or, alternatively, you're ready to go? This easy craft is quick and fun to make. Add your own image and message or use the templates in this book.

YOU WILL NEED:

- Card
- Paints
- Pens
- Glue stick
- Scissors

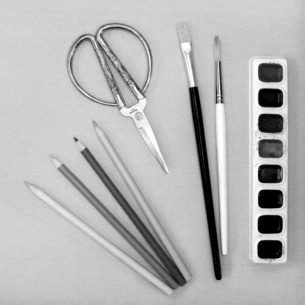

HOW TO MAKE YOUR DOOR HANGER:

1.

Take a piece of card and add a colorful wash of rainbow paint.

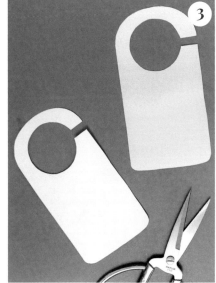

2.

Cut carefully around the hanger template.

3.

Cut out a second hanger from the card, facing the opposite way.

4.

Next, draw two Corgis: a sleepy one and a lively one!

5. Color and cut out the Corgi images.

6. Draw a little shadow under each image and stick it in place.

7. Stick the two signs back to back. Add an optional message: *Not Today* and *Let's Go!*

CORGI BALLOONS

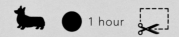 ● 1 hour ✂

Fun Corgi balloons are perfect for a party or as
a young family craft. So easy to make, each Corgi balloon
has its own personality. Use different colored balloons for
a fun selection and add a crepe paper ruff of hair.

YOU WILL NEED:

- Balloons
- Balloon sticks
- Paper
- Pens and pencils
- Crepe paper
- Scissors
- Glue stick

HOW TO MAKE
YOUR BALLOONS:

1.

Take a balloon and blow it up to a
medium size, about four puffs.
Attach a balloon stick to the base.

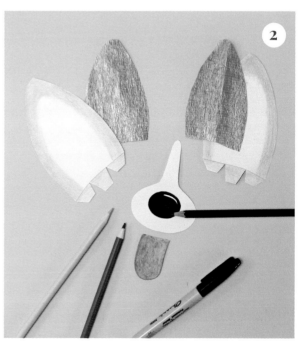

2.

Copy and cut out the templates
in this book or draw your own.
Color them in to make
the ear, nose, and tongue.

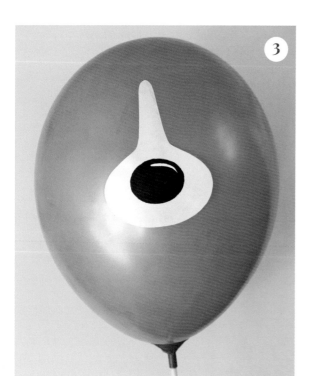

3.

Stick the nose to the
balloon with a glue stick.

4.

Next, add the tongue.

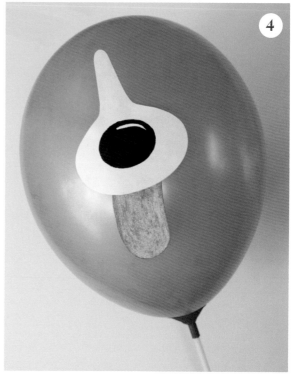

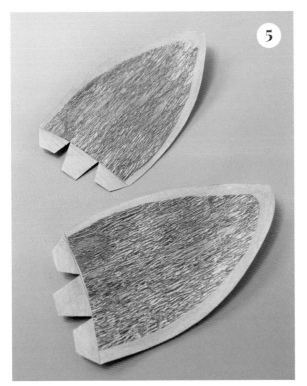

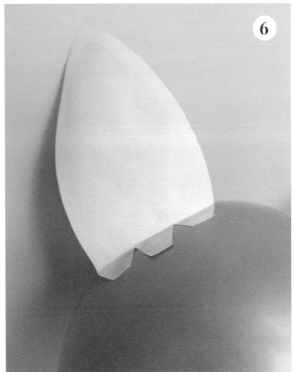

5.

Now to assemble your Corgi ears.

6.

Fold back the tabs and stick the ears to the ballon as shown.

7.

Take a Sharpie and draw your Corgi's eyes. Add some eyebrows too if you like.

8.

Now take some crepe paper in a similar tone and fringe cut one side.

9.

Wrap the crepe paper around the base of the balloon to create a ruff.

10.

Make lots of balloons in different Corgi colors!

CORGI POMPOM KEY RING

 ● 1 hour ✂

Make a DIY Corgi key ring with a pompom chest!
Choose any colored felt, from yellow to brown, for your Corgi.

Add a couple of tassels to your key ring and you are ready to go.

YOU WILL NEED:

- Felt in orange and white
- White yarn
- Card stock
- Key ring loop
- Ribbon
- Beads
- Needle and thread

HOW TO MAKE YOUR KEY RING:

1.

Use the templates in this book or create your own with card stock. Cut out the templates in orange and white felt.

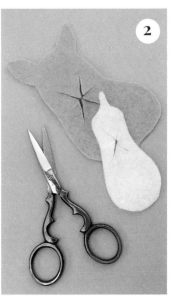

2.

Fold the felt Corgi templates in half to cut star shaped slits in each piece.

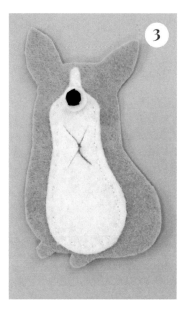

3.

Sew the white panel on top of the Corgi base. Add a small circular panel of white felt and a bead for the nose.

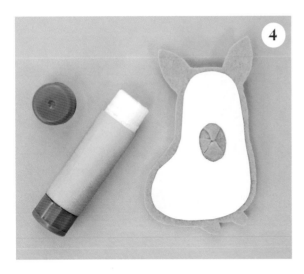

4.

Glue the white card in place
on the reverse of the panel,
using a glue stick.

5.

Now to make your pompom!
Wrap white yarn around three
fingers approximately 40 times.
Slip the yarn off your fingers
and carefully tie a length of
yarn around the center.

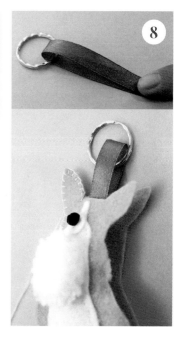

6.

Slip the yarn bundle through the hole in the felt pane, then cut through the loop on each side. You will now have a shaggy pompom.

7.

Trim your pompom front and back to make a neat Corgi chest.

8.

Loop a length of ribbon through the metal key ring. Place the loop between the two panels of felt.

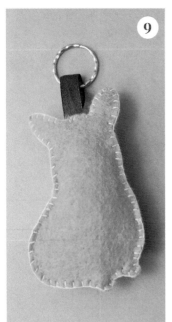

9.

Sew the two panel together using a blanket stitch.

10.

Add two small black beads for eyes. Stitch or glue them in place.

11.

You can also hang your Corgi key ring on your bag as a charm.

CORGI PAPER MASK

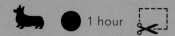 ⬤ 1 hour ✂

Snip and stick these easy 3D Corgi paper masks.
Add a paper crown for a touch of class. Make as many
masks as you like in different colors.

Perfect for a costume party or imaginative play time!

YOU WILL NEED:

- Card stock
- Colored pens, paints, or pencils
- Glue stick
- Scissors
- Ribbon

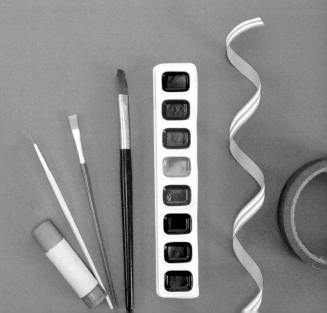

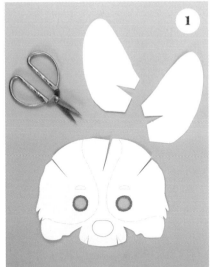

HOW TO MAKE
YOUR MASK:

1.
Copy the mask template in this book and carefully cut out the head, ears, and eyes.

2.
Color your mask using paints, pens, or pencils.

3.
Glue the middle panels together.

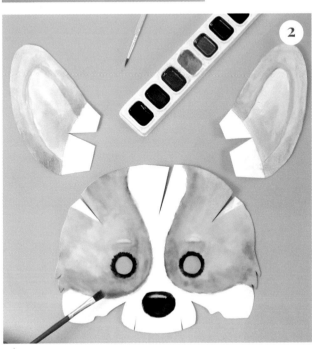

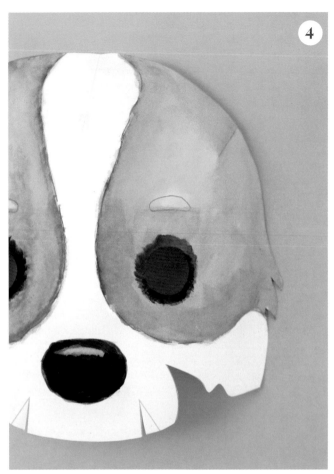

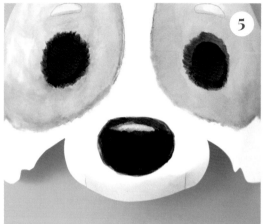

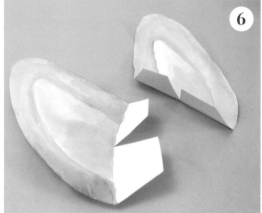

4.

Next, stick the two side panels together.

5.

Glue together the tabs at the bottom of the mask.

6.

Fold the tabs on the base of each ear.

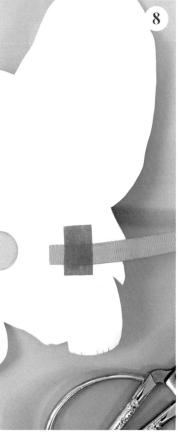

7.

Attach the ears to each
side of the mask.

8.

Lastly, add ribbon to
each side of the mask.

9.

Why not add a crown?
Follow steps in Project 1,
using paper instead of felt.

Set up a craft table and have some Corgi fun!

CORGI BOW TIE

 ● 1 hour

Spruce up your doggy's collar with a fun fabric bow tie.
Use colorful scrap fabric and follow these simple steps to
create an easy-to-wear bow tie for your poochie pal.

Luna the Corgi loved her bow tie and had lots of admirers.
What a dapper doggy!

YOU WILL NEED:

• Colorful fabric
• Needle and thread
• Scissors
• Ribbon

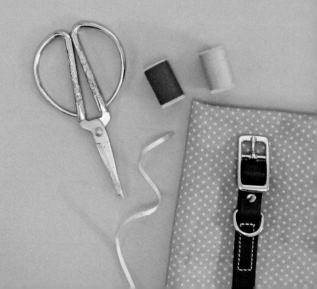

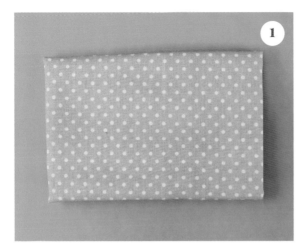

HOW TO MAKE
YOUR BOW TIE:

1. Choose a colorful fabric and fold widthwise then lengthwise to approxiately 6 × 7 inches.

2. Concertina fold the material in the middle to form a bow tie shape.

3. Wrap a long, thin strip of material around the center of the bow.

4. Secure on the back with a few stitches.

5. Add two loops of ribbon or elastic so that you can easily slip your dog's collar through the bow tie.

6. Doesn't Luna look smart and happy in her bow tie?

CORGI MINI BOOKS

 ● 1 hour ✂

Make your own miniature book with just a few sheets of copy paper. This technique is very simple. Build up a library of mini books and have fun coming up with creative covers.

Perfect as tiny notebooks, you can also attach them to a backpack or key chain by glueing a little ribbon in the book spine.

YOU WILL NEED:

- Copy paper
- Scissors
- Glue stick

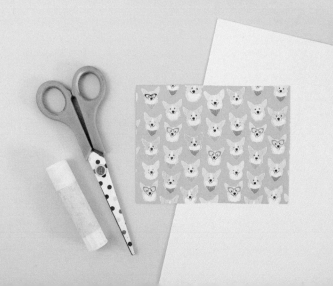

HOW TO MAKE YOUR MINI BOOKS:

1. Fold a letter-sized piece of copy paper in to four long strips.

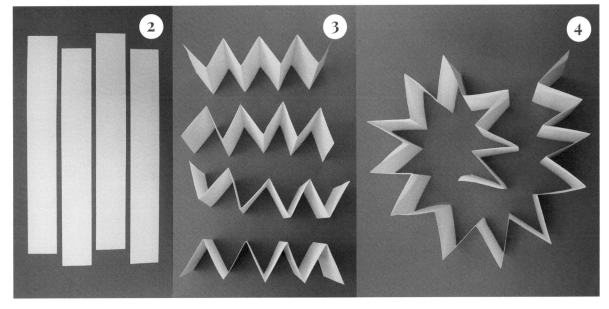

2. Cut the paper into four strips.

3. Concertina fold each strip as shown.

4. Join strips together to make one long zigzag.

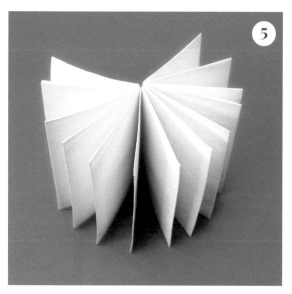

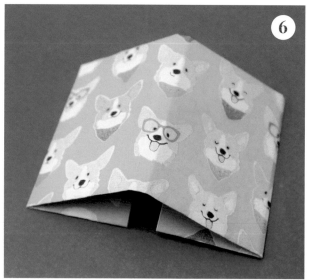

5. Starting at the left, glue the pages back to back, two at a time. Cut off the final spare page.

6. Fold the jacket as indicated on the template in this book.

7. Carefully slot the first and last pages in to the inside folds. Your mini Corgi book is ready.

TEMPLATES

In this section, you can find templates for some of the projects in this book. The templates are for tracing, scanning, or copying. Some should be resized to the right size for your project.

PROJECT 23: CORGI MINI BOOKS

fold fold fold fold fold fold fold fold fold

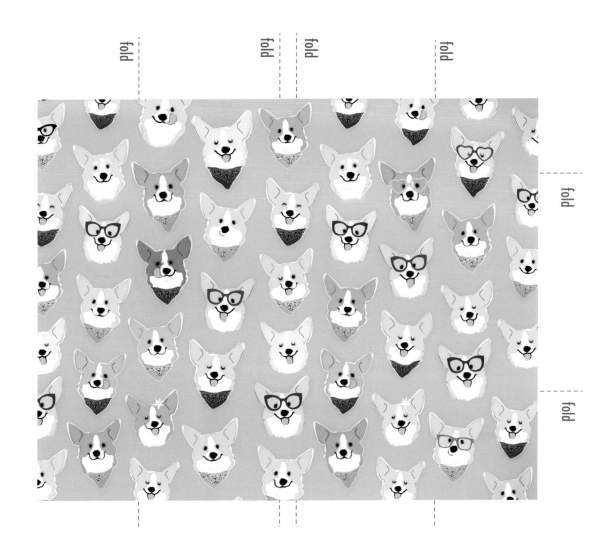

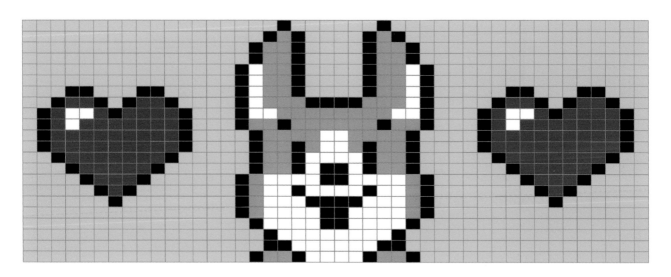

start weaving here

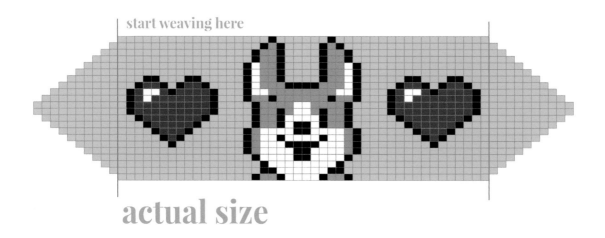

actual size

PROJECT 14: CORGI PLATES 1

PROJECT 1: CORGI CROWN

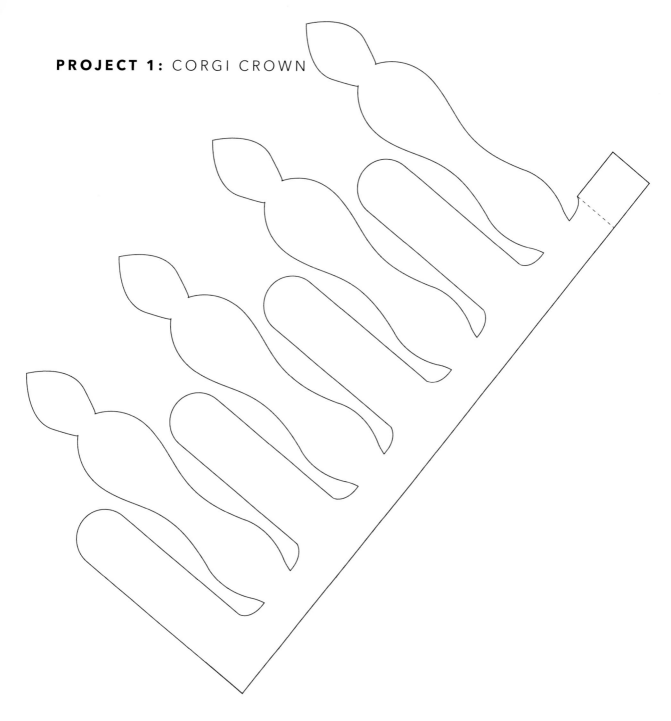

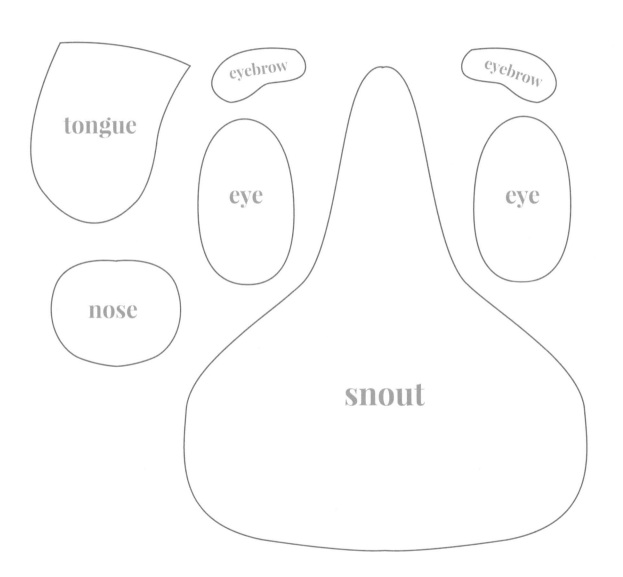

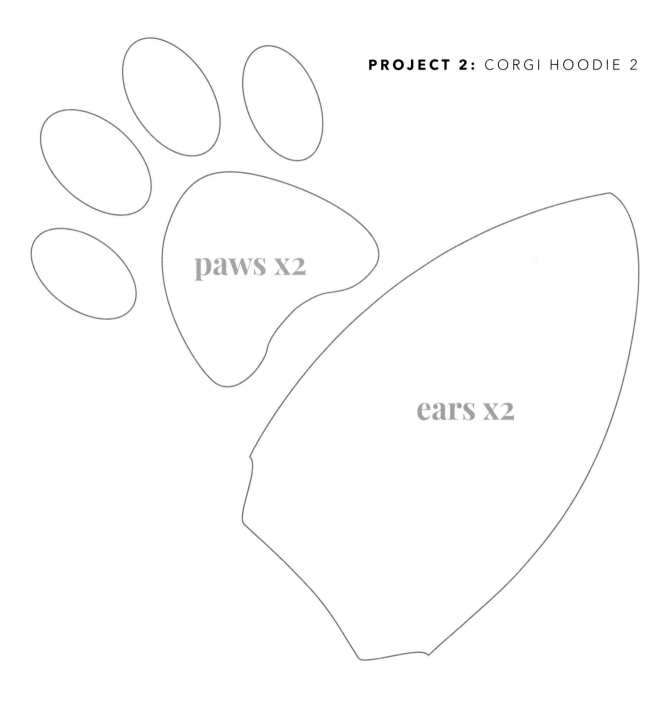

paws x2

ears x2

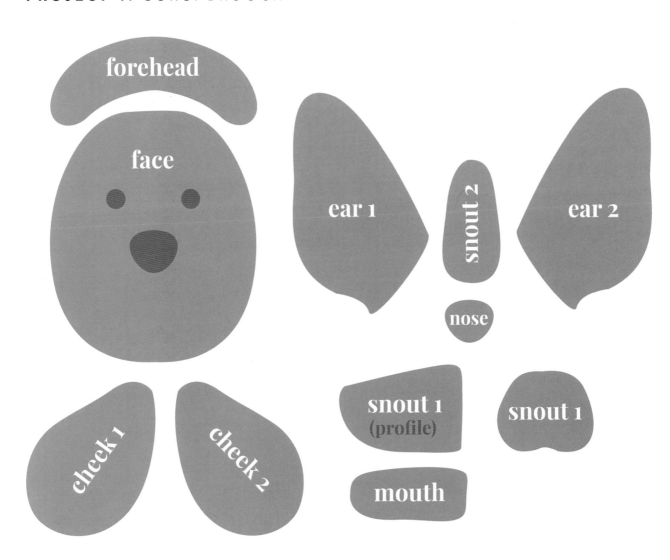

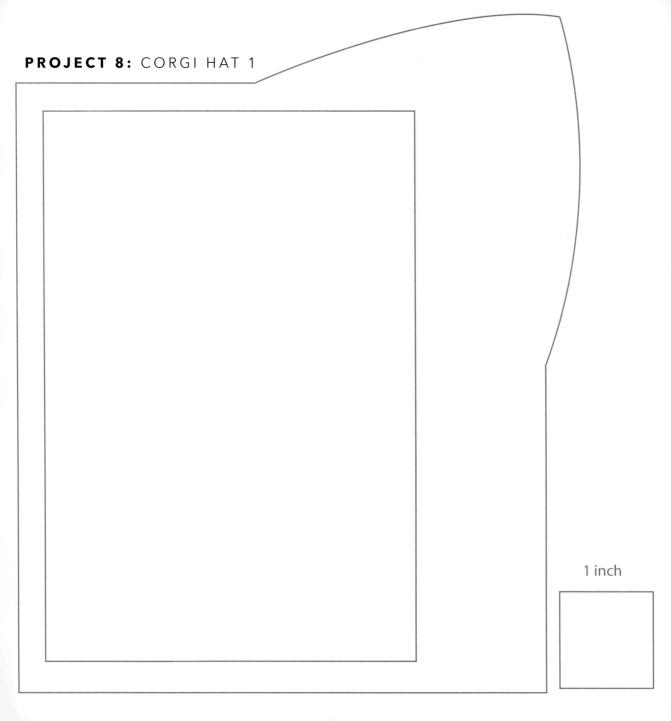

1 inch

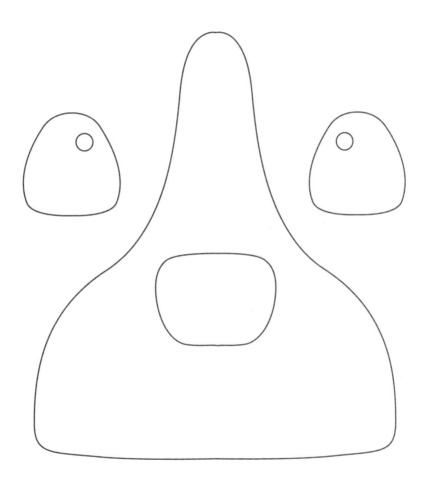

PROJECT 9: CORGI BOOKMARK

PROJECT 10: CORGI STRING ART

Scale template by 205%

PROJECT 11: CORGI CUSHION

Scale to desired size

PROJECT 12:
CORGI EYE MASK 1

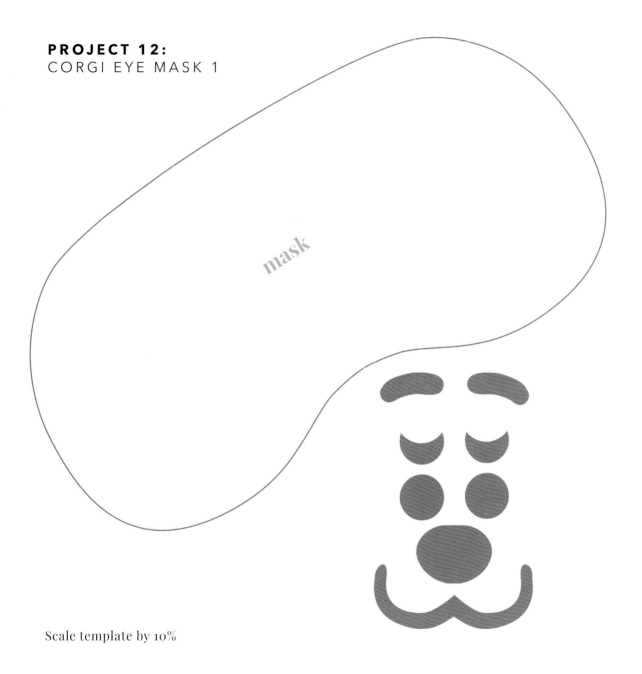

mask

Scale template by 10%

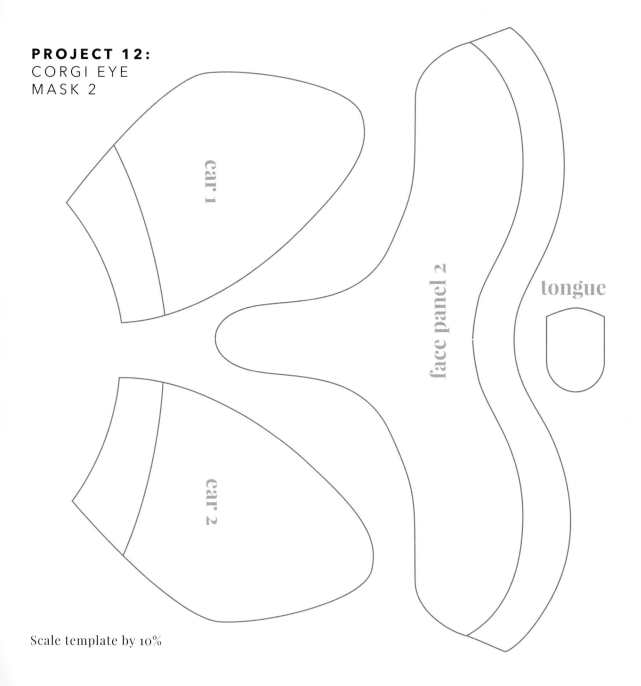

PROJECT 12:
CORGI EYE
MASK 2

ear 1

ear 2

face panel 2

tongue

Scale template by 10%

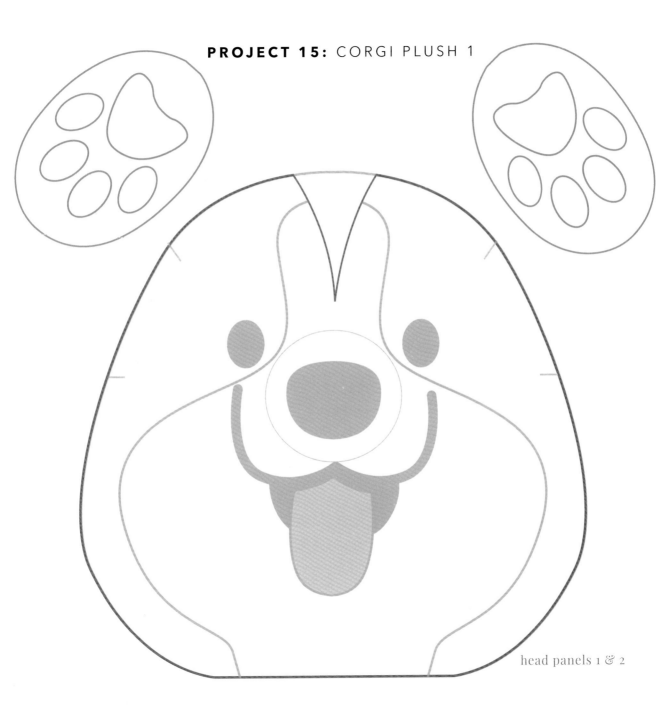

head panels 1 & 2

PROJECT 15: CORGI PLUSH 2

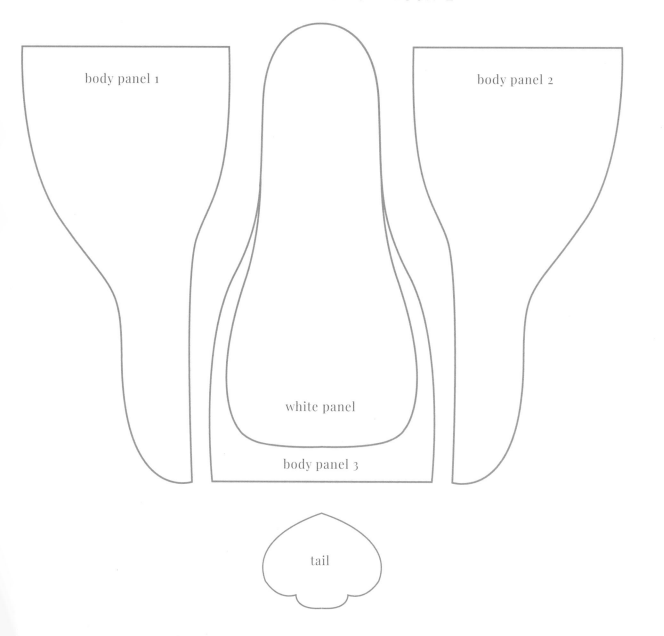

body panel 1

body panel 2

white panel

body panel 3

tail

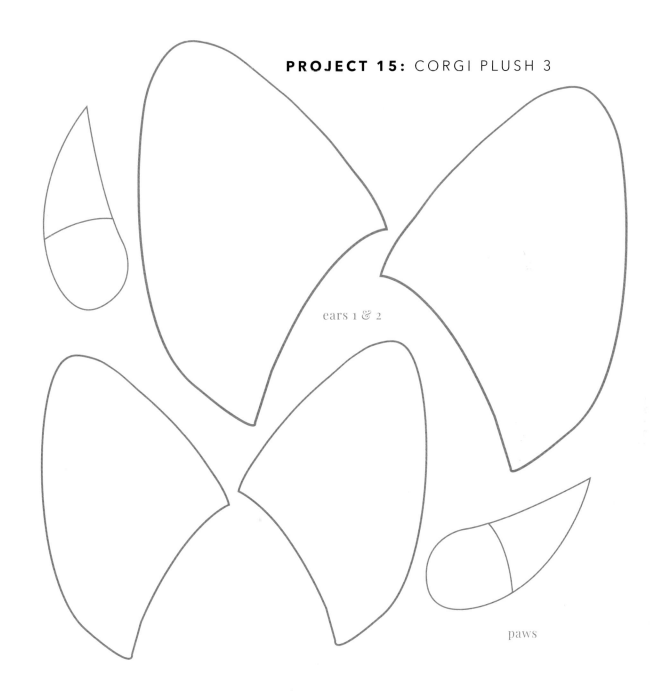

PROJECT 15: CORGI PLUSH 3

ears 1 & 2

paws

PROJECT 16: CORGI GIFT BOXES

PROJECT 18: CORGI DOOR HANGER

front

back

PROJECT 19:
CORGI BALLOONS

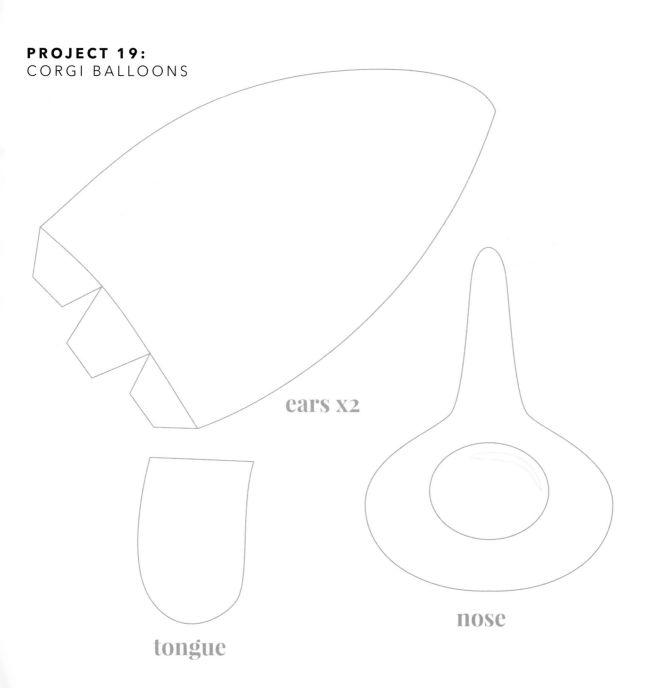

ears x2

tongue

nose

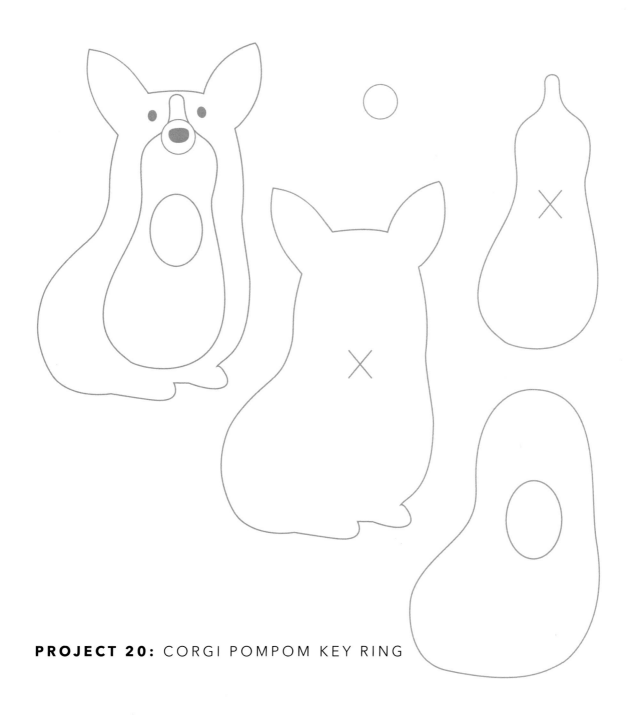

PROJECT 20: CORGI POMPOM KEY RING

PROJECT 21: CORGI PAPER MASK 1

Scale template by 115%

PROJECT 21: CORGI PAPER MASK 2

Scale template by 115%

WITH THANKS TO

Harvey and Missy, the inspiration for Happythought! Javiera Isabel Gallardo Varas, my partner in crafts. Our champion Corgi friends Holly and Lunita and their Corgi mama Yenifer Muñoz Caces (Queen Moon Corgi Chile). Milenko Ullrich Zulic & Allie. Our wonderful models Nachelle, Aaron, Ivan, Tilly, Missy, Julieta, and Maite. Julio Cid Mora, Jesse McHugh at Skyhorse Publishing, Rose Deakin for her Corgi research, and to all our family for their love and support.

CREDITS

Creative Direction: Ellen Deakin.
Design and Layout: Antonia Orrego Requena & Ellen Deakin.
Crafts: Ellen Deakin, Javiera Isabel Gallardo Varas,
Anahi Varas Barilla, Pedro Murua Bovio.
Photography: Diego Astorga Carneyro & Ellen Deakin.
Production: Harry Olden.

ALSO AVAILABLE

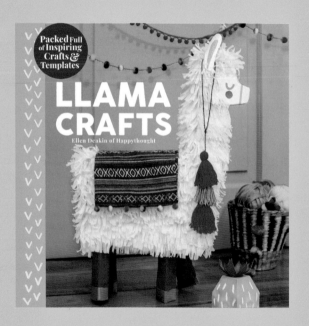

THE END...

ABOUT THE AUTHOR

An avid crafter since childhood, Ellen Deakin trained in design at the renowned Glasgow School of Art, then went on to work in the United Kingdom as a graphic designer, illustrator, and art director. In 2010, along with her husband Harry Olden, she launched Happythought, a craft website, full of inspiring ideas, tutorials, and projects.

At Happythought, the emphasis is on producing craft templates that, as well as being lovely to look at, are easy to make, with the minimum of fuss and the maximum of fun! Ellen is also the author of *Llama Crafts* and *Sloth Crafts*, two more craft books packed with ideas and inspiration.

You can find lots of fun craft projects, printables, and tutorials at happythought.co.uk.

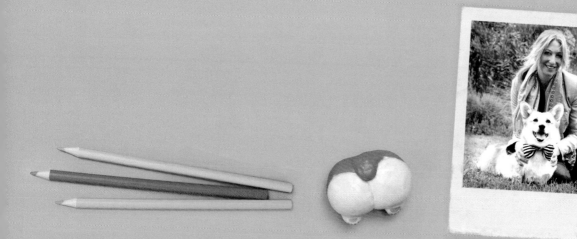